FRANKIE & ME

by Peter Fardell

edited by Alison Hedger

A happy musical about an ordinary girl's attempts to fin
at her new school. She discovers that you don't have to be **y.**

When you need a friend, the only monster is prejudice!

Suitable for KS2.
Younger children will also enjoy taking part in this musical.

Approximate duration: 45 minutes.

CD with demonstration and backing tracks included.

SONGS

1. Here Comes The New Girl
2. A Shiver Down My Spine
3. Proper Friends
4. W.E.I.R.D.
5. We Can't Believe Our Eyes
6. Frankie And Me

Reprise: A Shiver Down My Spine (2)

7. The Monster Shuffle
8. Does It Really Matter?

TEACHER'S BOOK complete with CD, production notes and music.

The script is in the separate Pupil's Book GA11451

A licence should be obtained from the publishers for performances of this work

A division of Chester Music Limited
8/9 Frith Street, London W1D 3JB

Order No. GA11440
ISBN 0-7119-9811-6

9.95

PRODUCTION NOTES

CAST LIST

*indicates solo singers

THE HUMANS

Mary Shelley*
A modern namesake of Frankenstein's original author. Mary is a kind and ordinary girl who builds monsters from papier-mâché.

Kevin
A boastful, arrogant boy. Friendly with Petunia.

Miss Teak*
A teacher with a penchant for ghoulish stories. She is slinky, looks "Gothic" with dark hair and pale skin and has a air of mystique about her.

Lewis*
A pleasant lad who needs a bit more courage.

Petunia
An unpleasant, bossy girl who eventually gets comeuppance for her cheating and bullying ways.

Sarah
An intelligent girl who is much put upon by Petunia. She finally comes into her own.

Dad*
Mary's good, but very absent-minded father. He is a scientific genius but misses most of what's going on around him.

Optional extra schoolchildren.

Optional extra white-coated scientists to help Dad in Song 4.

Optional Choir of children to bolster singing and to provide sound effects.
All dressed as monsters would be fun!

THE MONSTERS

Frankie
Big and with almost human form. Green-faced and scary, but very good-natured. Could be played by an adult if maximum height contrast is desired. Largest speaking part of monsters. Speaks five verses over musical backing in Song 7.

All the other monsters mainly feature in the reprise of Song 2 and in the dance at the party at the end of the musical. Extra requirements are listed below in brackets.

Bones
Beautifully spoken skeleton.
(lines in Scene 8 and leads the band in Scene 10)

William
Enthusiastic werewolf.
(Lines in Scene 8 and howls a bit)

Victor	Amiable vampire. (Walk-on part in Scene 9 and optional backing vocals in song 7)
Mirabelle	Nice ghost. (Walk-on part in Scene 9 and optional backing vocals in song 7)
The Mummy	Very, very old lady, well wrapped! (Non-speaking)
Mister Zombie	Run-of-the-mill living corpse. (Non-speaking)

Optional extra monsters for reprise of Song 7 and at the party.

PREJUDICE: SOME FACTS

Colour, creed, nationality, culture, size, lifestyle, class, accent, dress . . . the list of worthless reasons people find to discriminate against each other goes on. But 'friendship', that thing we all need when we are feeling lonely or frightened, has always been a priceless commodity. Asylum seekers are so much in the news lately that we have perhaps lost sight of the expression's true meaning. The dictionary defines asylum as 'refuge', 'shelter' or 'sanctuary', but sadly this is not always what our society offers newcomers. A survey by MORI has revealed that two-thirds of the nation's adults think that "there are too many immigrants in Britain" and about as many (63%) feel that "too much is done to help them". At the same time, the survey found that people grossly overestimate the number of refugees who are actually allowed to stay and the amount of financial aid that they can hope to receive. However, MORI also discovered that the younger generation are generally more tolerant than the over 65s and the degree of prejudice against any particular group decreases sharply if people actually know someone from that group. This last fact is hardly surprising. Only by getting to know one another will we build a happier world.

Families come into a new country, people moving to a new town or job, children starting at a new school: we are all asylum seekers. So let's not fear those we don't know yet because whilst we may all be different in some ways . . .

when you need a friend, the only monster is prejudice.

PROPS AND SCENERY

- A briefcase for Dad, with the initials W. E. I. R. D.
- Paper (for Mary's picture, Dad's report and Sarah's ghost story)
- Various kitchen things (teapot, milk carton, toast, plates, coffee pot *etc.*)
- A thermos flask
- A glass tumbler
- Green face paint
- A pastry brush
- Two lunch boxes
- A calculator
- A big dictionary
- A box labelled "Glasses"
- Dummy instruments for the monster band

Monster costumes, wigs, masks *etc.* can be made or brought in by the children. A white adult shirt makes a good laboratory coat on a child.

There are 10 scenes:

Scene 1	In School
Scene 2	The Street
Scene 3	Mary's Kitchen
Scene 4	Mary's Kitchen (next morning)
Scene 5	The Playground
Scene 6	Mary's Kitchen
Scene 7	Outside Mary's House
Scene 8	Mary's Kitchen (the following afternoon)
Scene 9	In School
Scene 10	Mary's House

Most scenes take place at school or in Mary's kitchen. The schoolroom speaks for itself but in the kitchen scenes various bits of scientific clutter (flasks, microscopes, textbooks *etc.*) should be lying around amongst the normal kitchen things, to reflect Dad's profession. In the play, Mary uses a pastry brush to paint Frankie's face and there's no reason why she can't really do this. Face paint might be better than ordinary paint though! The outdoor scenes do not really require scenery and can simply be performed without it or at stage front. The last scene should look like a party with balloons, streamers *etc.*

MUSIC AND DANCE

The choir could be dressed as monsters too. Optional harmony parts are indicated in the music. Solo singing parts could also be sung as a whole choir or small group. In Song 6, Mary and Frankie dance and/or play together to an instrumental repeat of the melody. This could include hopscotch, hat-swapping, hand-clapping games and whistling. *The Monster Shuffle* dance gives some individual monsters a chance to dance in the appropriate way during their verse (spoken by Frankie). Everyone should shuffle from foot to foot in the chorus. A swaying mass of monsters is the desired effect.

SONG ONE

HERE COMES THE NEW GIRL

All
(echo in Refrain and optional second part in Chorus)

Cue: Here she comes!

G7
C
Am
F
Em
Here comes the new girl.
Here she
optional harmony
(here comes the new girl,)
(Here comes the new girl. Here she

Dm/G
Dm/G
comes.
comes.)

C Em F G7 C Em F G7
1. Here's the new girl, we can see her now. What's the fuss? It's no big deal.
2. Does she know there's things she must-n't do, things which simp - ly should-n't be done?
3. Does she think she's some - how bet - ter for being the last to join our lot?
Here's the new girl, Here's the new girl,
C Em F G7 C Em F G7 C
Who said she could come here an - y how? No one asked us how we feel.
For her sake we hope she does-n't do an - y - thing to spoil our fun.
Well, let's nev - er ev - er let her for - get she's new and we are not!
Here's the new girl, Here's the new girl.

Chorus
F G7 C C7
unison
(All) She might not un - der - stand the rules we've made,
F G7 C G
She might do ev - 'ry - thing all wrong.
F G7 C C7
Well, if she blun - ders, then we're not a - fraid

F
D7
Dm/G
to send her back where she be - longs!
Last time to Coda
G7
Coda
C
Here comes the new girl.
ff

SONG TWO A SHIVER DOWN MY SPINE

Miss Teak + Children + All

Cue: . . . exciting and above all . . . SCARY!

G7 C A7 Dm G7
ghost-ly hand on mine!
(Tell me more!)
C B7 C
Send a spook-y sign!
(Yes please!)
Pet - ri - fy, e - lec -
A7 D9 G7
- tri - fy me, when I feel that shiv - er down my spine!

Children: (both times) Woo!
C F C C7 F
(You've got it!) (Remember . . .) Let the ten - sion build!
C Woo!
I want my flesh to creep!
F Woo! D7
I'll be more than thrilled if you nev - er let me sleep!

G7 C B7
(All together now!) All: Make my big eyes shine!
f
C A7 D9 G7
When I'm fright-ened, I'm en-light-ened! Got to feel that shiv-er down my spine!
1. 2.
C Dm G7 C C6
(well all right!)
ff

SONG THREE

PROPER FRIENDS

Mary + All

Cue: Friends! Oh I've loads of friends!

D
D7
G
Ground. Say "Hi" to Gar - den Wall. Oh,
aah. Aah - - - aah,
Em
A7
D
D
they're not pro - per friends at all. There's Hedge, who's ra - ther
aah - - a - ah. Aaa - - -
Em
A7
D
dense, and Tree who lives by Fence. They
aah, aaa - - - aah.

D7 G Em A7
make me feel so small. Oh, they're not pro - per friends at
Aaa - - - aah, aa - - aa -
D F B♭m F
all. Have you met Dust - y Lane? She's
ah. Aaa - aa - aah.
B♭m F B♭m
al - ways un - der my feet. And don't for - get Broth - er
Aa - aa - aah. Aa - aa -

1.
F
B♭
A
B♭
A
A7
Rain, he's of - ten fall - ing in my street. All: My
2.
F
B♭
A
B♭
A
Rain, he's of - ten fall - ing in my street. Who's
- aah. Aa - aa - aah - aah. Who s
D
Em
A7
this come home to rest? He's known as Lone - li -
this come home to rest? He's known as Lone - li -

D
D7
- ness. I hoped he would - n't
- ness. I hoped he would - n't
G
Em
A7
call, he's not a pro - per friend at
call, he's not a pro - per friend at
D
Solo
Em
A7
D
all . . . He's not a pro - per friend at all.
all.
mp

SONG FOUR

W.E.I.R.D.

Dad + other White-coated Men

Cue: Well now, how can I explain?

Grandly, with pomp ♩ = 120

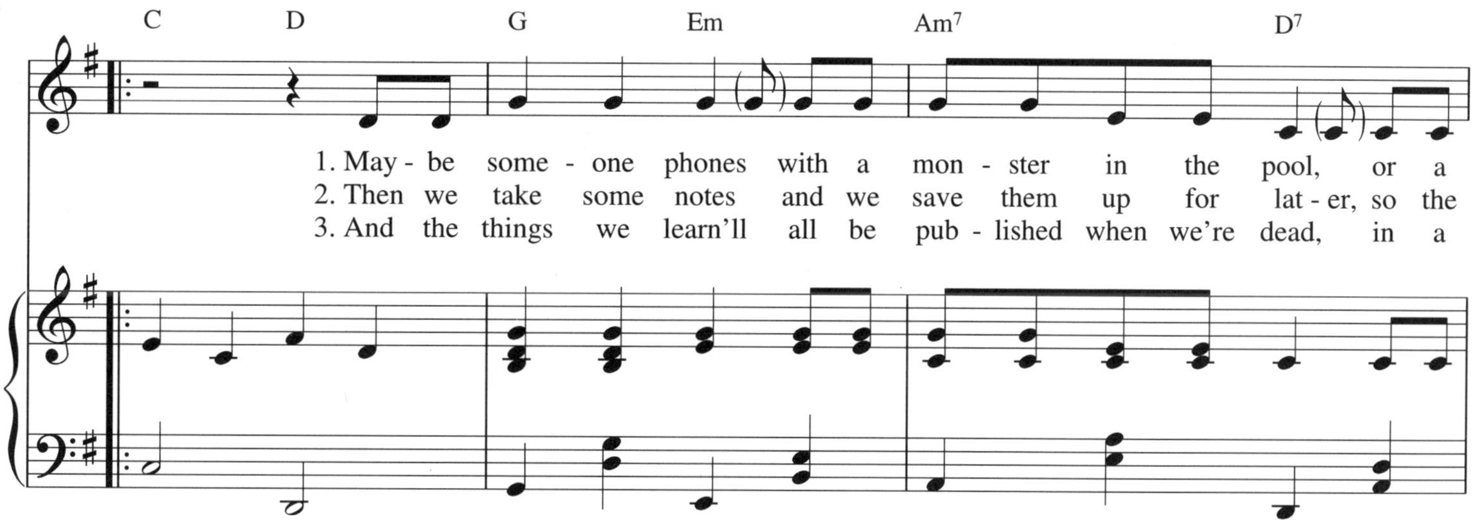

Gmaj7
Chorus
C C/B Am C/G
cel - lar full of bones or an at - tic with a ghoul,
men in white coats can get bu - sy with the da - ta.
fun - ny lit - tle jour - nal which is hard - ly ev - er read,
And we use ev - 'ry sci - en - tif - ic
Am Am/G D/F♯ G C D Em
gad - get we can get to re - solve all the an - swers to the ques - tions we've been set, at the
(Slower from 𝄋)
C C/B Am7 C/G D7/F♯ D G G/F♯ Em7 G/D
World - wide Ex - per - im - ent - al In - sti - tute, at the World - wide Ex - per - im - ent - al

E7 F#dim E/G# E7 C Am G D7
(note optional lower harmony part)
In - sti - tute for Re - search and Dis - cov - er -
1.2.
3.
4.
G
G
rall.
D.S. al Fine
G
Fine
- y. - y. At the - y.
rall.

SONG FIVE

WE CAN'T BELIEVE OUR EYES

Mary + Lewis
(divide verses as appropriate)
Cue: AAAAAAAAAAAAARRRRRGH!

Cm A♭7 Cm A♭7
can't be - lieve our look - ers, 'cause what they say has
can't be - lieve our eye - balls! They should have read their
Cm B♭ A♭ G
shook us, and though they swear there's some - thing there, we
bi - bles, 'cause then they might know wrong from right. We
INSTRUMENTAL SECTION
G7 Cm G
can't be - lieve our look - ers!
can't be - lieve our eye - balls!
(SCREAM!)

Cm G Cm Fm
(SCREAM!)
Gaug5
1.
2.
(SCREAM!)
3. We
(Repeat 1.) We
Coda
Cm G G7b9 G7add9 Gaug5 Cm6
eyes! We can't be - lieve our eyes!
8vb

SONG SIX

FRANKIE AND ME

Mary

Cue: Oh yes, best friends!

Gm C7 Gm C7 F
beau - ti - ful day, _ be - cause Frank - ie and me _ are such friends.
Gm C9 F Gm C7(add 9)
He's the one who makes things fun, stops me ev - er feel - ing
F A7 Dm
blue. Helps me find peace of _ mind, _ and I

1.
2.
G7
C
G7
know he feels the same way too!
Repeat is INSTRUMENTAL for DANCE
C7
C7aug5
F
D7
Gm
C7
We can laugh, we can shout, we can let it all out,_ and_ we
3
3
Gm
C7
F
D7
both feel so hap - py and free. If you're won - der - ing why_ there's no

Gm C7 Gm C7 Gm C7
sun in the sky, well don't come com - plain - ing, it's not real - ly rain - ing, the
Gm C7 Am7 D9aug5 Gm
sun is as bright as can be! It's shin - ing on
C7(add 9) F F7 Fdim7 B♭m6/F F C7aug5 F
Frank - ie and me!
8vb

SONG SEVEN

THE MONSTER SHUFFLE

Frankie (spoken, not sung) + All

Cue: Bones! Give us some music!

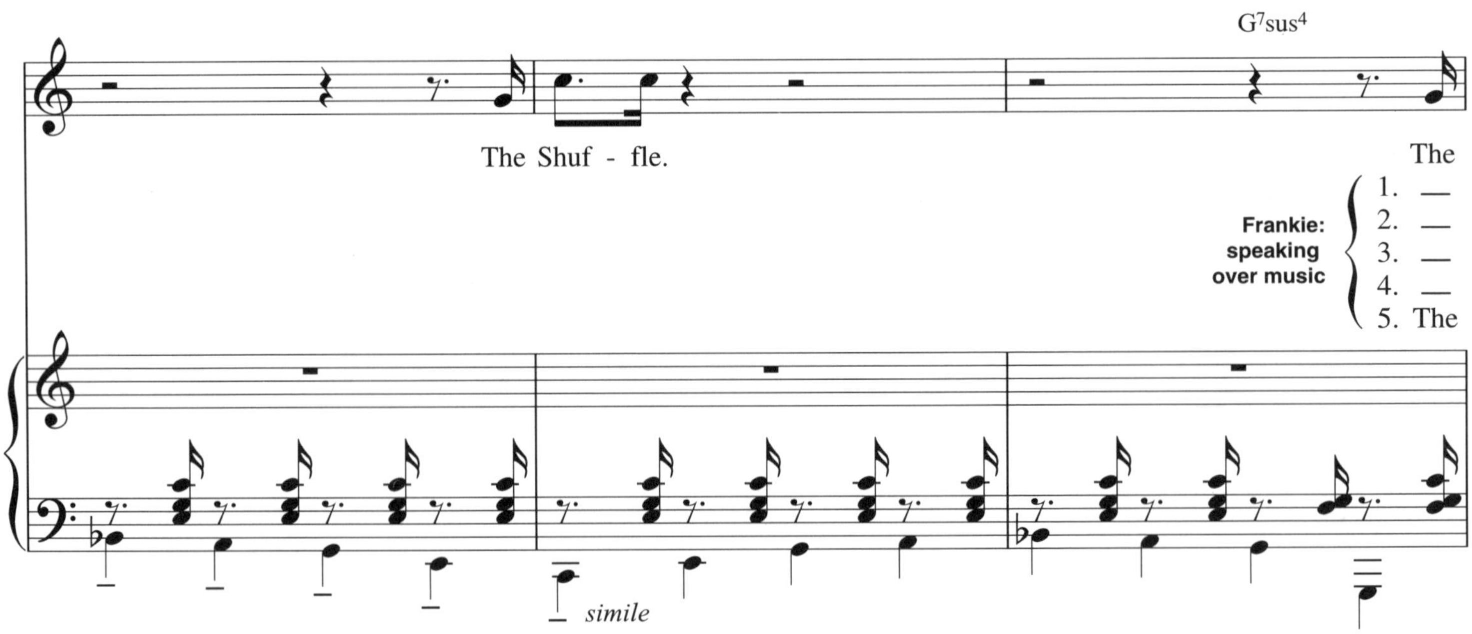

C7
Shuf - fle. The
Hi, my name is Frankie. To - night I'll be your host
Come on Mister Zombie, let's see you do your stuff.
William is a werewolf. I know he's kind of hairy, but
Mummy here is ancient, her skin is dry as parchment. She
rest of you are humans and you're not a pretty sight. I'd
Shuf - fle. The
Bones, there is a skeleton and Mirabelle's a ghost.
Was your grave too shallow, 'cause you're looking rather rough? Now
once you get to know him, he isn't all that scary. He
made the trip from Egypt where she's got her own apartment. She
really hate to meet you down an alley late at night! But to
F7
Shuf - fle. The
Victor is a vampire, he drinks blood to stay alive. We're
pull yourself together, and shake a leg my friend, I
howls like a dog, he's got a thing about the moon. I ex -
lives out in the desert in a pointy block of flats. Her
judge you by appearance, that would really be a crime. So come

D7 G7 C Gaug5
Shuf - fle, the Shuf - fle, the Shuf - fle.
doing the Monster Shuffle. Let's jive!
hope it won't drop off before the end!
- pect you'll all find out about it soon!
body's also home to several rats!
on and do The Shuffle, one more time!
Chorus
C6 G7♭9 G7
All: Do the Mon - ster Shuf - fle. Turn - ing up the heat now!
f
C6 G7♭9
Do the Mon - ster Shuf - fle! Can you feel the beat now?

C6
C7
F7
Do The Mon - ster Shuf - fle, and those who've had e - nough 'll
1.2.3.4.
C
G7♭9
C
take a lit - tle break and rest their feet! The
Last time
(no chords)
C7
feet!
Monster noises, including massive howl from William
8vb

SONG EIGHT

DOES IT REALLY MATTER?

All

Cue: Hit it, Bones!

D7
G
sort of clothes you wear? The coun - try where you come from or the
C
A7
G
C7
G
school that you at - tend? It real - ly does - n't mat - ter in the end.
2. Does it real - ly mat - ter if you're fat or thin?_ The food you like for din - ner or the

D7 G C A7
col - our of your skin? Do some peo - ple's voi - ces near - ly drive you round the bend? It
G C7 G Cm
real - ly does - n't mat - ter in the end. 3. Does it real - ly mat - ter if you
G C Cm G
don't all look the same? Does it real - ly mat - ter if you've got a fun - ny name?

C Cm G E7 A7 D7
If you think it mat - ters it's a cry - ing shame: it real - ly does - n't mat - ter at all!
1. 2. E♭7 A♭
4. Does it real - ly mat - ter if you
E♭7
op - en your heart? Make some - bod - y wel - come, may - be help them make a start?

A♭ D♭ B♭7 A♭ D♭7
Does it real - ly mat - ter if you try to be a friend? That's all that real - ly mat - ters in the
A♭ D♭7 A♭ E♭
end. That's all that real - ly mat - ters in the end. That's
ff
A♭ D♭7 A♭
all that real - ly mat - ters in the end.
8vb

CD Track Listing

Complete Songs (with vocals)

1. **Here Comes The New Girl**
2. **A Shiver Down My Spine**
3. **Proper Friends**
4. **W.E.I.R.D.**
5. **We Can't Believe Our Eyes**
6. **Frankie And Me**
7. **The Monster Shuffle**
8. **Does It Really Matter?**

Backing Tracks (vocals omitted)

9. **Here Comes The New Girl**
10. **A Shiver Down My Spine**
11. **Proper Friends**
12. **W.E.I.R.D.**
13. **We Can't Believe Our Eyes**
14. **Frankie And Me**
15. **Reprise: A Shiver Down My Spine (Song 2)**
16. **The Monster Shuffle**
17. **The Monster Shuffle: Alternative version of Song 7***
18. **Does It Really Matter?**

*Alternative version of Song 7: Includes Frankie's spoken part, but omits backing chorus.

Music Arranger
Rick Cardinali

Vocals
Heather Ramage
Mike Winsor

Recording Engineer
Jonas Persson

CD Recorded at Music Sales Limited
London W1